# THE TORS OF DARTMOOR

~~~~~~~~~~~~~~~~~~~~~~~~~~~~~~~~~~~~~~~~~~~

## Roy Egerton Downard

*Leedon Tor:* A large solitary granite rock with peripheral remains.

This version of the book is virtually as originally published, presenting the work of Roy Egerton Downard. There are now additional pages at the back providing information about the publisher, Arthur L Clamp.

**Please note that some of the information has changed since this book was first updated. An addendum that provides an update is included towards the end of the book. The addendum was compiled by Paul Rendell, local historian and editor of Dartmoor News.**

The republishing project is being managed by Arthur's grandson, Steven Gibson. We aim to find all the research that he was involved in publishing, preserving it for the next generation as part of 'The Clamp Collection'.

# INTRODUCTION

DARTMOOR has fascinated people for centuries and many excellent books have been written on this subject including Samuel Rowe's, *Perambulation of Dartmoor*, Crossings, *Dartmoor*, and Worth's, *Dartmoor*, with many others. Extending over an area of 430 square miles it presents pictures of beauty and grandeur, wastes and wilds, coombe and tors. Inhabited a thousand years before the Christian era, relics of those days are in evidence in the many and various stone circles, standing rows, menhires, pounds, kistvaens and hut circles all of which are spread widely across the moor.

Also will be discovered the remains of mines from which have been extracted silver, lead, tin and copper, and these activities together with quarrying have in the more recent centuries considerably altered the character of the moor in many places. On Dartmoor there are more than 150 tors, ranging from High Willhayes, with a height of 2,038 feet, to some which are only large hills and which are nevertheless called tors. All these tors are contained in an area of the 440 square miles and which is 22 miles long from north to south and 20 miles wide from east to west.

Dartmoor has an area known as the *Dartmoor Forest*, not because of the existance of vast areas of trees, but its use as a hunting area. It also gives source to many rivers, brooks and streams, some little known and others so well known as to give name to prominent towns: River Dart and Dartmouth, the River Teign and Teignmouth, the River Plym and Plymouth and the River Tavy and Tavistock.

So many visitors to the moor associate it only with the prison, and Princetown is a rendezvous for the curious. To a large number, however, the interest in Dartmoor is in the tors and rivers and great delight is found in the scenery, the wild animals and the stone remains. It has to be remembered that so much of the moor can only be visited on foot, but the sight of the wild ponies, sheep and cattle grazing in quite unexpected places is a reward for the effort involved.

The annual "round up" of the wild ponies in which hundreds of them are driven off the moor to centres, one of which is near Yelverton, is a sight well worth seeing, and what a pleasure it is to find oneself resting in an isolated spot and to have at hand whortleberries which grow in profusion during the summer months. Also the heathers give immense colour to the moorland and those seeking white heather will find it in the area of Corndon Tor.

Remembering that Dartmoor can be both docile and inhospitable, those intending to visit the interior are offered the following words of caution.

*Have regard to weather conditions and wear suitable clothing and footwear. If intending to stay more than a day acquaint someone on your intentions. If unaccompanied do not venture too far into the Moor.*

*If possible carry a compass. Remember the hazards of fogs, bogs and marshes.*

*Take suitable provisions — there are no shops in the heart of the Moor.*

*Beware of training areas where red flags are displayed, live ammunition may be in use. Consult local newspapers for firing times.*

*It is unlawful to feed the ponies.*

*Avoid mine shafts.*

*Leave the Moor as you expect to find it, in other words take your litter away with you.*

The author originally became interested in Dartmoor and its tors through exercising his labrador. Walking with his dog he traversed large areas not seen from the roads and tracks, and he has never ceased to be amazed at the unending variety of beauty to be found. To stand in the middle of Dartmoor with tors at all points of the compass and with not a sign of human activity or work in any direction leaves one sharing the same view with the inhabitants of two thousand years ago and it is an inspiring sensation. A lifetime is not nearly long enough to appreciate the characteristics of this wonderful Dartmoor and the more one sees the more one wishes to discover. This book is intended to be an aid to those similarly interested.

Roy Egerton Downard,
Wembury Point, South Devon.

**ARCH TOR**  
*Height above sea level: 1340 feet*  
*Ordnance survey reference: 635782*

Situated very close to the Two Bridges to Postbridge road, it is one and a half miles South-West of Archerton. East of the tor will be found a wooded area in the centre of which is an enclosed hut group and a stone circle.

**ARMS TOR**  
*Height above sea level: 1450 feet*  
*Ordnance survey reference: 541864*

Dominated by the Great Links Tor to the east it forms part of the military firing range and is one mile east of Shartacombe on the Tavistock to Okehampton road. The River Lyd passes its western slopes whilst another tributary rises to the south of it. Hut circle remains can be found to the north, east and west and a cairn to the east. It is approached by a track to the east of the Fox and Hounds inn at Shartacombe, and passing the Nodden Gate the Arms Tor will be reached. Notice must be taken of red warning flags to indicate military firing before entering the Moor.

**BAGGA TOR**  
*Height above sea level: 1220 feet*  
*Ordnance survey reference: 556806*

Situated about three miles east of Mary Tavy, it is subject to use by the military authorities. Hut circles will be found on the eastern slopes. It is reached by road from Mary Tavy to Wapsworthy, then by a moorland track to the base of the Tor. This is a minor tor in east Dartmoor. One mile to the south west there will be found the remains of a cairn, an enclosure and hut circles. It is approached from Ashburton by taking a road north to Ruslade, then to the hamlet of Bagtor which is on the southern slopes of Bogtor.

**BEARDOWN TORS**  
*Height above sea level: 1680 feet*  
*Ordnance survey reference: 605775*

Located in central Dartmoor it has a clitter top. There are remains of enclosures and hut circles on the eastern slopes. The old Devonport Leat passes between it and Longford Tor. The tor is in a danger area and should not be approached when warning flags are flying. It is approached from Two Bridges, following the Devonport Leat upstream to the east side of the tor.

*Brat Tor:* Surmounted with a cross commemorating Queen Victoria's Jubilee.

**BEETOR**  
*Height above sea level: 994 feet*  
*Ordnance survey reference: 708843*

This tor lies on the very edge of north east Dartmoor, is not of great height or importance as far as historic remains are concerned, in fact the nearest hut circle remains are more than a mile west. It will be discovered three miles west of Moretonhampstead on the Plymouth road, and a cross will indicate the tor just to the north.

**BEL**  
**TOR**  
*Height above sea level: 1115 feet*  
*Ordnance survey reference: 695724*

Situated north-west of Ashburton it stands above the very steep and lovely banks of the River Dart which area is noted for its outstanding beauty. It is easily accessible and following the winding road north-west from Ashburton to Spitchwick, Bel Tor is less than a mile ahead.

**BELL**  
**TOR**  
*Height above sea level: 1348 feet*  
*Ordnance survey reference: 729778*

Not a very significant tor, it is found on eastern Dartmoor, it has a clitter top and rock basins are to be found. It is approached from Widecombe in the Moor, about one mile north east of the village and the road from Widecombe to Bonehill passes the bottom slopes.

**BELLEVER**  
**TOR**  
*Height above sea level: 1456 feet*  
*Ordnance survey reference: 644765*

About a mile east of a point five miles from Tavistock on the Moretonhampstead road a tributary of the River Dart passes through its lower slope and to the west of it. Hut circles and a kistvaen can be found in the immediate vicinity. On the south-western side will be found a stone mass of logan stone formation in which a huge piece of granite is raised above the rock formation and balances in such a manner that it is possible to move it. Superb views of the immediate moorland can be had from the summit.

**BELSTONE**  
**TOR**  
*Height above sea level: 1567 feet*  
*Ordnance survey reference: 613920*

This northern Dartmoor tor has many interesting features. Remains of a barrow are located on its slopes and many hut circles are found here and also on Belstone Common. The tors which encircle the common and particularly Belstone Tor are littered with granite slabs known as *clatters*. Also interesting are the Cullever Steps and Irishman's Wall to the south. It is approached from the hamlet of Belstone and is subject to use by the military authorities.

**BENCH**  
**TOR**  
*Height above sea level: 1060 feet*  
*Ordnance survey reference: 685717*

Close to the lovely wooded Dart valley. It is half a mile north of the Venford Reservoir. Hut circles exist to the east and west and it is approached from Hexworthy by following the road to Holne past the reservoir. The tor is then to the north.

**BIRCH**  
**TOR**  
*Height above sea level: 1550 feet*  
*Ordnance survey reference: 685814*

This tor is east of the road between Postbridge and Moretonhampstead, and on it will be found the remains of a burial ground; a disused mine exists to the south. It is located by the ancient Bennett's Cross standing by the side of the road a half a mile west of the *Warren House Inn*. Birch Tor is immediately to the east of the cross and eight hundred yards from the road.

*Black Tor:* Moorland ponies grazing between the large granite stones.

**BLACK**  
**DUNHILL**
*Height above sea level: 1615 feet*  
*Ordnance survey reference: 582775*

Is in an area where many historic remains can be found. Enclosures, hut circles and a stone row, whilst to the west is a tumuli. It is easily accessible and midway between Two Bridges and Rundlestone will be found a long straight road to the north and about a mile long; this ends at the base of the hill. Black Dunhill is in a danger area and the usual precautions should be taken.

**BLACK**  
**HILL**
*Height above sea level: 1916 feet*  
*Ordnance survey reference: 605846*

This tor is deep in the heart of Dartmoor and is one mile south of the well-known Cranmere Pool. The East Dart river passes by the eastern slope of the hill. It is in a danger area and the usual precautions should be taken as regards warning flags. The best approach is from Okehampton proceeding south and uphill past the railway station and on to the moor, past the Army camp on the right, and follow the moorland road to its most southerly point. A walk of about three miles in a southerly direction is now necessary and Cranmere Pool will be part of the tor area.

**BLACK**  
**TOR**
*Height above sea level: 1137 feet*  
*Ordnance survey reference: 574718*

A lesser tor and one of several with this name it is found just three miles from Princetown on the road to Yelverton. There are remains of hut circles and an enclosure; also a logan stone and a stone row are within easy reach of the main road.

**BLACK**  
**TOR**
*Height above sea level: 1100 feet*  
*Ordnance survey reference: 679637*

This tor is located in the south part of Dartmoor and is part of Brent Moor north of South Brent. It has remains of hut circles, an enclosure and a stone row. It is reached from South Brent by a road which follows the river north to Shipley Bridge. Black Tor rises steeply at this point.

**BLACK** *Height above sea level: 1485 feet*
**TOR** *Ordnance survey reference: 568895*

Another of the three tors with the same name. It has a clitter top which is evidence of volcanic action in much earlier days. It is a mile west of High Willayes which is Dartmoor's highest tor, and is in a danger area used by the Army for firing and other practices. Attention should be taken of warning red flags. It is found by taking a moorland track half a mile south of the *Sourton Down Inn* which will lead to the West Okement river. Black Tor will then be half a mile to the east.

**BOG** *Height above sea level: 1050 feet*
**TOR** *Ordnance survey reference: 763757*

A lesser tor at almost the most easterly part of Dartmoor. There are several approach roads depending on what part of the county one is situated in. Ashburton is well known and would be a good starting point. Proceed north to Rushlade then on to Horridge and Bagtor. Bog Tor lies about half a mile from Bagtor.

**BOULTERS** *Height above sea level: 1350 feet*
**TOR** *Ordnance survey reference: 525782*

Situated in west Dartmoor it commands excellent views for a full half circle extending to Cornwall and South-West Devon. It has a clitter top and remains of hut circles and enclosures are to be found in the vicinity. The tor is easily accessible from Peter Tavy and a track leads across the tor.

**BRANSCOMBE** *Height above sea level: 1750 feet*
**LOAF** *Ordnance survey reference: 552890*

Situated in North-West Dartmoor it is just off the Tavistock to Okehampton road. It has a cairn or burial spot on the northern slope and to the east will be found slipper stones. Access to Branscombe is best from Sourton where a moorland track east will skirt around Sourton Tors and between the latter and Shelstone Tor a steep climb will lead to "Loaf".

**BRAT** *Height above sea level: 1510 feet*
**TOR** *Ordnance survey reference: 539857*

Standing in North-West Dartmoor this tor provides a splendid panoramic view from its peak over East Cornwall and North Devon. It rises steeply from the Mary Tavy and Okehampton road and starting at the *Dartmoor Inn* on this road, a moorland track leads east to the top of the tor. It is a danger area and the usual precautions should be observed.

**BRENT** *Height above sea level: 1008 feet*
**TOR** *Ordnance survey reference: 474805*

Quite a unique tor inasmuch as a small church rests on its summit. There are several legends connected with the church and one is that a mariner said he would build a church on the summit of the highest piece of ground visible from the English Channel. About four miles from Tavistock on the Lydford road the tor will be plainly visible on the eastern side of the road. This tor attracts so many visitors that a convenient car park has been provided and will be found at the base of the tor.

**BUCKLAND** *Height above sea level: 1281 feet*
**BEACON** *Ordnance survey reference: 736731*

One of several tors in close proximity and it is about three miles north of Ashburton. It is noted for its view point and from the top of the Beacon spectacular views can be enjoyed of the River Dart valley and surrounding woods. The remains of a hut circle can be found on the eastern side. A road from Ashburton to Buckland in the Moor will lead to the base of the Beacon.

**BUTTERN**  
**HILL**
*Height above sea level: 1350 feet*  
*Ordnance survey reference: 655887*

This is an interesting tor three miles west of Chagford. To the east of the hill are a number of hut circles, a kistvaen and to the south will be found the Scorhill stone circle, whilst to the north is to be found a stone indented with a cross. A road from Chagford through Murchington to Gidleigh Castle brings one to within one mile of Buttern Hill.

**CALVERSLAKE**  
**TOR**
*Height above sea level: 1450 feet*  
*Ordnance survey reference: 608676*

Standing at the source of the River Plym it is in an area known as "Plym Steps". Of interest is the Abbotts' Way, a well worn track made by monks many years ago in crossing the moor from Buckfast to Tavistock and which passes Calverslake on the east side. On its slopes can be found the remains of a cist and an enclosure. Access is best from Dousland on the Yelverton to Princetown road and to Sheepstor. A right hand turn after passing the church and going east will find the road ending at a ford. Proceeding on foot past the old Eylesborough Mine the tor will be seen to the south east. It will be necessary to cross the River Plym to reach it and the Abbotts' Way can be used for this purpose.

*Brent Tor:* Very well known for the church on its summit.

**CAWSAND**  
**BEACON**
*Height above sea level: 1750 feet*  
*Ordnance survey reference: 635915*

Situated at almost the extreme north of Dartmoor it is only one and a half miles south of Sticklepath on the Okehampton road. A stone row and hut circles are to be found on the eastern side whilst a cairn exists on the summit. The River Taw flows on the eastern side. From Sticklepath a track to Skaigh Warren to the south will lead to the northern slopes of the Beacon.

**CHAT**  
**TOR**
*Height above sea level: 1774 feet*  
*Ordnance survey reference: 555854*

Situated in North-West Dartmoor it has a clitter top and an unusual arrangement of laminate bedding of stone slabs as though placed by human hands. At the base of the tor and to the east runs the Rattlebrook and within the area can be found a disused mine. It is not easily accessible but following the River Lyd from Beardon on the Tavistock to Okehampton road to its source will lead to the base of Chat Tor and also that of Doe Tor.

*Crockern Tor:* Site of the very old Stannary Parliament.

**CHINKWELL**  
**TOR**

*Height above sea level: 1252 feet*  
*Ordnance survey reference: 729782*

Standing in East Dartmoor it provides a splendid view of the land to the south. It has a clitter top and remains of hut circles can be found there. It will be necessary to use several minor roads to reach the tor and from Moretonhampstead follow the road west for three miles to Hele Cross turning right to Holwell Lawn which lies at the foot of Honeybag Tor and Chinkwell Tor.

**COMESTONE**  
**TOR**

*Height above sea level: 1106 feet*  
*Ordnance survey reference: 671718*

Also known as Cumsdon Tor it is a mile south of Dartmeet and the wooded valley of the Walla Brook. This area is a favourite beauty spot and at Dartmeet car parking facilities are provided. Hut circles will be found on all sides of the tor and to the south-east is the Venford Reservoir. It is easily approached from Dartmeet as a pathway south leads direct to the tor.

**CONIES DOWN**  
**TOR**

*Height above sea level: 1650 feet*  
*Ordnance survey reference: 587792*

Stands just north of the litchway or path from Petertavy to Lydford Tor, whilst the Cowsic River flows on its eastern side. It has a double stone row and hut circles are to be found to the south. The tor can be approached from Two Bridges on the Princetown to Moretonhampstead road and by following the River Cowsic upstream. It is in a danger area and the usual precautions should be observed.

**COOMSHEAD**  
**TOR**

*Height above sea level: 1080 feet*  
*Ordnance survey reference: 588688*

About two miles east of Sheepstor village it has a clitter top, hut circles and an enclosure whilst to the north will be found a stone row and a cairn. Eylesborough Mine, one of the last to be operated in the district, lies to the east and a rock known as the "Cuckoo Rock" is prominent on the west side. It is approached from Dousland thence to Sheepstor village and two miles east will bring one to the end of a path and a further mile will have to be made across the moor.

| | |
|---|---|
| **CORNDON TOR** | *Height above sea level: 1415 feet*<br>*Ordnance survey reference: 687743* |

The tor is situated north-east of Dartmeet on the Two Bridges Ashburton road and rises directly from the road to its clitter peak. On its summit will be found a tumulus or burial ground and has the appearance of a long pile of small rocks and stones. It is easily approached from a point two miles west of Dartmeet where a track to the north will lead to the tor.

| | |
|---|---|
| **COX TOR** | *Height above sea level: 1450 feet*<br>*Ordnance survey reference: 531762* |

When leaving Tavistock for Princetown it is the most prominent to be seen and is about three miles from the former. The view from its highest point is remarkable and provides a mirador of many miles particularly west towards Cornwall. It is noted for its barrows and stone rows. It is subject to use by the military and notice should be taken when warning flags are flown. It is adjacent to the road and access is easy.

| | |
|---|---|
| **CRAMBER TOR** | *Height above sea level: 1411 feet*<br>*Ordnance survey reference: 584712* |

Situated in the south-east of Dartmoor it is just east of the Yelverton to Princetown road. The slopes and valley to the west are rich in prehistoric remains and hut circles, enclosures and a cairn can be found. It can be located four miles from Yelverton on the above mentioned road and at which point Cramber Tor will be observed about one mile to the west.

| | |
|---|---|
| **CRIPTOR TOR** | *Height above sea level: 1030 feet*<br>*Ordnance survey reference: 556727* |

A tor of not great significance it is less than one mile from the Walkham River. It is found by passing through Walkhampton (a mile north of Dousland) to Eggworthy where a moorland track leads to the tor.

| | |
|---|---|
| **CROCKERN TOR** | *Height above sea level: 1428 feet*<br>*Ordnance survey reference: 614757* |

This is the tor where Stannary Parliaments were held and the stannary towns of Tavistock Plympton, Ashburton and Chagford sent burgesses as representatives. The Stannary legislators found the tor so cold and exposed at times that after the swearing in of the jurors the Court reassembled at one of the stannary towns. The West Dart River flows a quarter of a mile away, and hut circles and an enclosure are to be found there. It is easily accessible and about one mile north of Two Bridges and half a mile west of the road the tor is found.

| | |
|---|---|
| **CROW TOR** | *Height above sea level: 1600 feet*<br>*Ordnance survey reference: 607787* |

Situated in mid-Dartmoor it is not of importance, not having any particular characteristics, or prehistoric remains except that of a kistvaen. It is not easily accessible and Two Bridges is the nearest point from which the tor can be reached. Following the Devonport leat north past Wistman's Wood with Beardon Tors on the right, Crow Tor will be reached two miles from Two Bridges. It is in a danger area and usual precautions should be taken when warning flags are flown.

| | |
|---|---|
| **CUT HILL** | *Height above sea level: 1980 feet*<br>*Ordnance survey reference: 598827* |

This is one of the highest hills on Dartmoor and is about two miles from Cranmere Pool. A stream known as Combe Water rises on the west side as also do many other brooks. It is not easily accessible and there are no tracks to follow. A suggested route starts from Okehampton, proceeding uphill past the railway station and on to the moor, going through the moor gate and following the road south to its end, it will now be necessary to proceed on foot due south for about three miles. It is in a danger area and the usual precautions should be taken when warning flags are flown.

**DEVILS TOR**  *Height above sea level: 1751 feet*
*Ordnance survey reference: 595797*

Situated in mid Dartmoor it is not very accessible. It is noted for the "Beardown Man" a menhir or vertical stone erected in prehistoric times. It is a stone of great weight and is nearly twelve feet high. Also in the area is a kistvaen. A southerly approach is the best from Two Bridges following the course of the Cowsic River to its source for about three miles and Devils Tor will be discovered on the right hand side of the Cowsic. It is in a danger area and usual notice should be taken of warning flags.

**DINGER TOR**  *Height above sea level: 1838 feet*
*Ordnance survey reference: 583883*

Located on the very high ground which forms part of High Willhayes. It has clitter on the summit, and is part of the Army training area. Access is best from Okehampton using the road which runs south and uphill past the railway station and on to the moor. Proceed through the moor gate and follow the road for about one mile then, taking the right hand fork, this will lead to Dinger Tor.

**DOE TOR**  *Height above sea level: 1524 feet*
*Ordnance survey reference: 545848*

It is to be found in the north-west of Dartmoor and is very prominent when viewed from the west. The tor has clitter formation on its peak and kistvaen remains. Approach it from the Tavistock to Okehampton road and from the *Dartmoor Inn* near Lydford where a moorland track to the east leads to Doe Tor Common and Doe Tor to the east. It is in a danger area and the usual precautions should be taken when warning flags are flown.

**DOWN TOR**  *Height above sea level: 1201 feet*
*Ordnance survey reference: 579695*

This tor has a clitter top and interesting prehistoric remains. On the eastern side can be found a cairn, hut circles, an enclosure and a stone row all of which are in close proximity. To reach this tor Burrator must be located, and the north part of the road which follows the reservoir brings one immediately to the west of the tor.

**EASDON TOR**  *Height above sea level: 1439 feet*
*Ordnance survey reference: 729824*

On the eastern edge of Dartmoor it is on the high ground west of the River Bovey providing an excellent view point. It has remains of hut circles and a cairn. The map makes mention of a "Whooping Stone" and this was probably a logan stone which has been regarded by some as an enchanted rock. Using the road from Moretonhampstead west to Two Bridges it is easily found. At Cross Hele three miles on this road a turning to the left will lead direct to the west side of the tor.

**EASTERN TOR**  *Height above sea level: 1019 feet*
*Ordnance survey reference: 584663*

Situated on the northern side of the River Plym it is in an area rich in prehistoric remains. Hut groups, stone rows, cairns and enclosures are plainly visible. It has a clitter top but is not of significant height. There is plenty of evidence of mining in the area and the disused Eylesborough mine to the east was one of the last to function in Devon.

It is easily located and starting from Dousland on the Yelverton to Princetown road proceed to Sheepstor village. Follow the road east until a ford is reached, a turning to the right will then lead to Warren House and the Eastern Tor.

**EAST MILL**  
**TOR**
*Height above sea level: 1683 feet*  
*Ordnance survey reference: 601902*

This tor lies between the Black-a-Yen brook and the East Okement River. An interesting cleavage in the rock formation is to be found here. Access is best from Okehampton to the moor past the railway station, through the moor gate and proceeding south for about two miles. It is in a danger area and note should be taken of warning flags when flown.

**FEATHER**  
**TOR**
*Height above sea level: 1120 feet*  
*Ordnance survey reference: 534742*

A minor tor situated three quarters of a mile south of the Tavistock to Princetown road. A cross erected here indicates that a path from Heckwood Tor to Whitchurch passes through this point. It is found by following the road from Tavistock to Princetown and at the top of a very steep hill three miles from the former a parking place will be found from which excellent views can be had. Feather Tor is half a mile south of the car park.

**FLAT**  
**TOR**
*Height above sea level: 1655 feet*  
*Ordnance survey reference: 605807*

Situated right in the heart of Dartmoor it is of little importance historically and must be considered as one of the minor tors. It is not easily accessible, but a track from Postbridge ends at Archeton and two very difficult miles will have to be covered on foot in a north-westerly direction.

**FOX**  
**TOR**
*Height above sea level: 1300 feet*  
*Ordnance survey reference: 623698*

Is in an area from which many water ways become rivers such as the Swincombe, Strange, Avon and the Plym. On the northern slope is Child's Tomb, and it is reputed that in order to shelter from the extreme cold Childe of Plymstock disembowelled his horse to hide in the carcass, but was nevertheless frozen to death. Just west is the Abbotts' Way and a cross will be found on its western side. Mining was carried on in the past and tinners' gullies are evident. Access is best from Princetown by taking the moorland road east to Tor Royal and then south to Nun's Cross. The summit of the tor is then about one mile to the east.

*Down Tor:* This is the site of many prehistoric remains.

| | |
|---|---|
| **GER TOR** | *Height above sea level: 1450 feet*<br>*Ordnance survey reference: 548832* |

This tor is in north-west Dartmoor and its eastern side falls rapidly to the River Tay and is known as the Tay Cleavage. On its western side can be found remains of hut circles and an enclosure. It is approached by following a moorland track past the Willsworthy Camp on the Tavistock to Okehampton road. One mile from the main road the track leads past White Hill and upwards in a south-east direction to the top of the tor. It is a danger area and note should be taken when warning flags are observed.

| | |
|---|---|
| **GIBBET HILL** | *Height above sea level: 1158 feet*<br>*Ordnance survey reference: 503812* |

Also known in some areas as Black Hill it has a commanding view of the country to the west and it is the most westerly part of Dartmoor. An ancient burial ground is there, but one would need to go east to find other remains of past human occupation. It is easily located as a track one mile north of Mary Tavy on the Tavistock to Okehampton road leads direct to the hill.

| | |
|---|---|
| **GIDLEIGH TOR** | *Height above sea level: 1088 feet*<br>*Ordnance survey reference: 673877* |

This is in a wooded area about two miles west of Chagford and rises just south of the hamlet of Gidleigh. It has several rock basins caused by ice and other weather conditions. The north River Teign flows through its lower wooded slopes and it is easily approached from Chagford via Gidleigh.

| | |
|---|---|
| **GREA TOR** | *Height above sea level: 1332 feet*<br>*Ordnance survey reference: 756783* |

Situated at the most easterly part of Dartmoor it has a clitter top and hut circle remains are to be found on the high ground. A logan stone is on the west side and cairns to the north-east. To the south is the old disused granite quarry railway. The tor is reached from Bovey Tracey and following the road west to Haytor Vale the old railway track can be found. A mile along this track and across Haytor Down Hill will lead to Grea Tor.

| | |
|---|---|
| **GREAT KNEESET TOR** | *Height above sea level: 1863 feet*<br>*Ordnance survey reference: 588859* |

The well known Cranmere Pool lies just east of its peak and Black Ridge Brook rises to the south-east. It is also noted for its peat pass. The tor is best approached from Okehampton by proceeding south and uphill to the moor, passing through the moor gate and following the road to its most southerly point; Great Kneeset is one mile and a half further south over the moor. It is in a danger area and notice should be taken when warning flags are flown.

| | |
|---|---|
| **GREAT LINKS TOR** | *Height above sea level: 1924 feet*<br>*Ordnance survey reference: 551868* |

Situated in north-west Dartmoor it has a clitter top and is visible from the Tavistock to Okehampton road. A cairn existed south of the summit and the Rattlebrook runs between it and Gren Tor. It is reached by starting at the *Fox and Hounds Inn* at Shartacombe. A moorland track leads to Nodden gate and, following the track north for a mile and a half, it suddenly turns south then a further mile leads to disused works. Great Links is then immediately south. It is in a danger area and note should be taken of warning flags when flown.

| **GREAT MISTOR** | *Height above sea level: 1768 feet*  *Ordnance survey reference: 562770* |

Lying just north of a point midway between Tavistock and Two Bridges it is one of the highest peaks in mid Dartmoor. It has a clitter top and is rich in prehistoric remains; tumuli, hut circles, an enclosure and a rock basin can be found. The River Walkham flows in the valley at the western base of the tor. It is approached by following the Walkham upstream from Merrivale on the above mentioned road for a mile and the tor is reached. The tor is in a danger area and notice should be taken when warning flags are flown.

| **GREAT NODDEN** | *Height above sea level: 1429 feet*  *Ordnance survey reference: 538875* |

On the north-west side of Dartmoor it is interesting for the cairns and hut circles in its area. The tor commands a splendid view to the west towards Lifton and Launceston. It is easily reached by following a track east from the *Fox and Hounds* near Bridestowe Station for two miles and it will pass near the peak of Great Nodden.

*Gutter Tor:* Storm clouds gathering above this well known outcrop.

| **GREEN TOR** | *Height above sea level: 1700 feet*  *Ordnance survey reference: 562864* |

Situated in the north-west of Dartmoor it is in an area of very high ground. It has a clitter top and the *Bleak House* ruin in Rattle Brook is just to the west. To find it start at the *Fox and Hounds Inn* at Shartacombe on the Tavistock to Okehampton road. A moorland track starts here and runs east to the Nodden Gate. Follow the track north for a mile and a half when it suddenly turns south and another mile leads to disused works and Green Tor is just south. It is in a danger area and notice should be taken of warning flags when flown.

| **GREN TOR** | *Height above sea level: 1650 feet*  *Ordnance survey reference: 551879* |

A very minor tor in north-west Dartmoor and stands under the shadow of the much higher ground to the east. It is mainly noted for a logan stone to the east. Access is best from the *Fox and Hounds* at Shartacombe on the Tavistock to Okehampton road. A moorland track going east leads to the Nodden Gate where another track north for two miles with a sharp turn south-east will lead to Gren Tor.

**GUTTER TOR**  *Height above sea level: 1149 feet*
*Ordnance survey reference: 577667*

Situated one and a half miles south-east of Sheepstor village and five miles from Yelverton. There are interesting rock formations and at the summit a rock basin can be found. These basins are thought to be man made. From the summit can be seen the River Plym running through the Ditsworthy Warren area and mine workings are apparent to the east. It is found by proceeding from Burrator to Sheepstor village and after passing the church turn right and continue east along the road until a brook straddling the road is reached; Gutter Tor is then immediately on the right and to the south.

**HAMELDOWN BEACON**  *Height above sea level: 1697 feet*
*Ordnance survey reference: 788708*

A tor by comparison if not by name lies south of the Two Bridges to Moretonhampstead road at a point four miles from the latter. Remains of cairns, a kistvaen and two barrels can be found and an excellent view of the south towards Ashburton can be enjoyed. At Shipley Common and at a point mentioned above a minor road runs south and three miles along this road will find the Beacon on the left hand side, that is to the east.

**HAMELDOWN TOR**  *Height above sea level: 1289 feet*
*Ordnance survey reference: 703806*

In east Dartmoor it is part of a long ridge stretching to Hookney Tor two miles to the north. It has a clitter top and on it can be found cairns and two barrows. Approach it from Widecombe in the Moor by taking the road north to Bagpark which stands on the eastern slopes of the tor.

**HAMERTON HILL**  *Height above sea level: 1289 feet*
*Ordnance survey reference: 562906*

To be found in north-west Dartmoor it is on the eastern side of the West Okement River. A moorland track about one mile north of Sourton on the Tavistock to Okehampton road leads east to the moor and the lower slopes of the hill.

*Great Mistor:* This very large tor is noted for its rounded rock formations.

## HANGSTONE HILL

*Height above sea level: 1983 feet*
*Ordnance survey reference: 615863*

It is one of the highest points on Dartmoor, has a clitter top, and a cairn can be found. Several rivers have their sources here. Immediately to the west is the well known Cranmere Pool and its letter box where one posts a letter and passes on any letters already there to a recognised Post Office, whilst the deposited letter is hopefully collected and posted by the next visitor. It does seem to work. Access is best from Okehampton. Proceed south and uphill past the railway station and on to the moor. Proceed through the moor gate and follow the road south to its end where a track leads direct to the hill. It is in a danger area and notice should be taken of warning flags when flying.

## HARE TOR

*Height above sea level: 1743 feet*
*Ordnance survey reference: 551843*

Standing in north-west Dartmoor it provides an extensive view of the west towards Lydford and Launceston in Cornwall. It has a clitter top, a barrow and hut circles on its slopes. The tor is visible from the Tavistock to Okehampton road and a track from Willsworthy Camp leads past White Hill and midway between Sharp Tor and Hare Tor to the south. It is in a danger area and notice should be taken when warning flags are flown.

## HART TOR

*Height above sea level: 1345 feet*
*Ordnance survey reference: 582720*

This tor lies just east of Walkhampton Common on the Yelverton to Princetown road and it is one of the smaller tors. Hut circles, cairns and an enclosure can be discovered. It is very close to the road and at a point one mile from Princetown it will be found on the east side of it.

## HARTLAND TOR

*Height above sea level: 1350 feet*
*Ordnance survey reference: 642798*

Situated less than one mile north of Postbridge on the Two Bridges to Moretonhampstead road it commands very fine views over the Postbridge area. The East Dart River runs past the bottom of its western slopes and another tributary of the Dart is on its eastern side. Standing stones will be found on the tor. It is easily reached from Postbridge and a track will lead to the tor.

## HARTOR TORS

*Height above sea level: 1341 feet*
*Ordnance survey reference: 603674*

This tor twins with Calverslake Tor in south Dartmoor, and is in an area known as "Plym Steps" and from where the River Plym starts its comparatively short run to the sea. On the southern slopes will be found the remains of hut circles, a cairn, enclosures and a double stone row. Access is from Dousland through Sheepstor village, and following the road east to the old Eylesborough Mine for two miles. Hartor will be seen to the south-east and it will be necessary to cross the River Plym to reach it. Actually the old Abbotts' Way crossed the river just north of the tor and it is still possible to use this crossing.

## HAYTOR

*Height above sea level: 1490 feet*
*Ordnance survey reference: 752768*

The area of Haytor is a well known beauty spot and is much visited. An imposing rock formation is seen and a rock basin and hut circles can be found to the north. A road from Bovey Tracey to Haytor Vale leads direct to the tor, a distance of four miles.

## HUCCABY TOR

*Height above sea level: 1400 feet*
*Ordnance survey reference: 657740*

A tor of lesser importance it is one mile west of Dartmeet. To the north are remains of hut circles and the Huccaby Ring, whilst to the north at the base of Laughter Tor exists a stone row. It is easily found as the tor is adjacent to the road between Two Bridges and Dartmeet and a mile from the latter.

**HECKWOOD TOR**  
*Height above sea level: 1050 feet*  
*Ordnance survey reference: 537738*

Visible from the Tavistock to Princetown road it is situated just west of the Walkham River which flows past its lower slopes. South of the tor will be found rock basins which are assumed by authoritarians to be hollows cut in the rocks to hold rain or dew. The tor is best approached from Sampford Spinney three miles north of Yelverton, and a track leads to the lovely Heckwood and to the Tor.

**HEN TOR**  
*Height above sea level: 1350 feet*  
*Ordnance survey reference: 593653*

This tor has an unusual amount of clitter which extends well down its sides. There is plenty of evidence of prehistoric activities here and hut circles are numerous. Willing's Wall and an enclosure within a pound can be traced. It can be approached from Yelverton by proceeding to Burrator and Sheepstor Village. Follow the road east to the disused Eylesburrow Mine. When a ford is reached a turning to the right and below Gutter Tor leads to Ditsworthy Warren, and almost due south across the River Plym lies Hen Tor and one mile from the river.

*Haytor:* The most well known of Dartmoor's tors.

**HICKTON HILL**  
*Height above sea level: 1400 feet*  
*Ordnance survey reference: 672667*

It is situated in an area with numerous hut circles and cairns, and just to the north will be found an extensive length of stone row. South will be found the Avon reservoir. From Buckfastleigh proceeding westwards to Cross Furzes then to Lud Gate two tors to the west will be seen; Hickton Hill is the one to the south.

**HIGH WILLHAYES**  
*Height above sea level: 2038 feet*  
*Ordnance survey reference: 579893*

The highest peak in the south of England and provides an extensive view of Cornwall to the west and Devon to the north. On its western side and north slopes there are cairns. To the north is Yes Tor the second highest peak on Dartmoor. To get to the tor start at Okehampton and proceed uphill past the railway station and on to the Moor. Enter through the moor gate and across the Moor Brook, follow the moorland road for a mile when a branch road to the right will be seen, follow it for another mile and High Willhayes will be on the right hand side. It is in a danger area and notice should be taken of warning flags when flown.

## HIGHER TOR

*Height above sea level: 1500 feet*
*Ordnance survey reference: 613916*

This tor twins with Belstone Tor and is reached in the same manner. To the north will be found the Cullever Steps and the Irishman's Wall. The River Taw passes on its eastern side. It is approached from the hamlet of Belstone, one and a half miles from Sticklepath on the Okehampton to Exeter road.

## HIGHER WHITE TOR

*Height above sea level: 1722 feet*
*Ordnance survey reference: 617788*

Situated in mid Dartmoor it is not noted for prehistoric remains, although further to the south-east hut circles can be found. It can be reached from Two Bridges and following the Devonport leat upstream and passing Wistman's Wood, a further mile north will lead to the western side of the tor.

## HOCKINGTON TOR

*Height above sea level: 1080 feet*
*Ordnance survey reference: 696717*

Its slopes rise steeply from the River Dart and from the peak splendid views of the wooded areas of the river can be obtained. The road from Two Bridges passing through Dartmeet to Ashburton is within less than a mile of the tor at Poundsgate and from which to the west easy access is possible.

## HOLWELL TOR

*Height above sea level: 1450 feet*
*Ordnance survey reference: 751777*

Situated in east Dartmoor it lies at the end of an old disused tramway which served the granite quarries in the neighbourhood. It has a clitter top and on the western side can be found hut circle remains. It is best reached from Bovey Tracey by taking the road to Haytor Vale and following the line of the tramway which ends just north of the tor.

## HOLLOW TOR

*Height above sea level: 1555 feet*
*Ordnance survey reference: 569747*

This is a very minor tor with few characteristics and has only a slight amount of clitter at the top. It lies half a mile south of the Tavistock to Princetown road at Rundlestone and is easily accessible.

## HONEY BAG TOR

*Height above sea level: 1450 feet*
*Ordnance survey reference: 727788*

Situated in east Dartmoor it twins with Chinkwell Tor to the south of it. Hut circles are to be found to the west. It is necessary to use several minor roads to reach the tor and from Widecombe in the Moor a road north for a mile and a half passes Honeybag Tor on its western side.

## HOOKNEY TOR

*Height above sea level: 1598 feet*
*Ordnance survey reference: 698814*

This tor lies between Birch Tor and King Tor in east Dartmoor and is also known as Hooknor Tor. Remains of hut circles can be found to the north of Shapley Tor which together with Hookney forms part of the high ground culminating with Hameldown Beacon two miles to the south. The whole area is rich in prehistoric remains and stone rows, barrows and cairns can be located. It is best reached from the Tavistock to Moretonhampstead road at Moorgate four miles east of the latter. A track south leads to the lower slopes of Shapley and Hookney Tors.

*Leather Tor:* A good example of a clitter formation.

**HOUND**  
**TOR**

*Height above sea level: 1469 feet*  
*Ordnance survey reference: 628890*

A clitter topped for it is most interesting inasmuch as at the top there are huge piles of granite as high as seventy feet, and a kistvaen and hut circle can be found on its slopes. Access is best from Okehampton using the road south and uphill past the railway station and on to the moor. Passing through the moor gate and following the track for three miles then a trek south and around Sheeperton Tor will lead to Hound Tor.

**HUNTERS**  
**TOR**

*Height above sea level: 1062 feet*  
*Ordnance survey reference: 762825*

Situated in east Dartmoor it rises steeply from the River Bovey and commands very good views over the surrounding countryside. The remains of an old camp exists and a clapper bridge will be found to the north western side. It is approached from Bovey Tracey on the Moretonhampstead road and at Wray Barton a turning west will lead to the clapper bridge mentioned above and which stands within easy reach of the tor to the south.

**INGRA**  
**TOR**

*Height above sea level: 1220 feet*  
*Ordnance survey reference: 555722*

A rather insignificant tor and noted for the reason that the old Princetown railway ran at its base. Between it and Leedon Tor to the south can be found an enclosure and hut circles. Following a road from Yelverton to Walkhampton and thence to Eggworthy an old track to the tor can be found.

**KENNON**  
**HILL**

*Height above sea level: 1569 feet*  
*Ordnance survey reference: 644895*

This tor is located in north-west Dartmoor, it has a clitter top and hut circle remains can be found to the east whilst a stone circle exists to the west. It can be approached from Whiddon Down on the Exeter to Okehampton road by taking a road south through Throwleigh to the moor. A ramble of less than a mile to the west will bring one to the tor.

**KESTOR**  *Height above sea level: 1432 feet*
*Ordnance survey reference: 665864*

Situated in west Dartmoor. On its western side can be found the remains of a triple circle, stone rows and a cist. Iron Age remains have been discovered in the area and an interesting rock basin is to be seen. The tor can be reached from the Teign basin starting from Chagford and proceeding to Teigncombe. A track from this hamlet will lead directly to the tor.

**KING**  *Height above sea level: 1636 feet*
**TOR**  *Ordnance survey reference: 709815*

To be found in east Dartmoor it is not to be confused with Kings Tor near Princetown. It has a barrow or burial mound known as Kings Barrow and to the north remains of hut circles. To reach the tor follow the road west for three miles to Cross Hele, and a turning to the left and one mile south Ganna Park is reached. Here at the crossroads a road to the left leads to Lower Hookney from which King Tor is visible.

**KINGS**  *Height above sea level: 1312 feet*
**TOR**  *Ordnance survey reference: 558734*

A prominent tor visible from the Tavistock to Princetown road and is in a commanding position above the River Walkham at Merrivale. The old railway track made a semi-circular turn around the higher part of the tor. To the north stone rows, hut circles and stone circles can be found. At a point one mile east of Merrivale can be found a road running south which serviced a quarry. Here will be found the railway track and following it west will lead to the tor from which magnificent views can be enjoyed.

**KITTY**  *Height above sea level: 1910 feet*
**TOR**  *Ordnance survey level: 567874*

A prominent tor in west Dartmoor, it has a clitter top and on the southern slope a logan stone. The West Okement River flows past its eastern slope. Bleak House ruins and disused works are to be found in the valley to the west. A moorland track from the *Fox and Hounds Inn* at Shartacombe on the Tavistock to Okehampton road leads east to the Nodden Gate, and a mile and a half north will end on Bridestowe Common. The track then suddenly turns completely to the south and leads to Kitty Tor. It is in a danger area and notice should be taken of warning flags when flown.

**LAUGHTER**  *Height above sea level: 1318 feet*
**TOR**  *Ordnance survey reference: 653756*

Is situated in mid Dartmoor. It has a clitter top, a double stone row and hut circle remains to the north and west. It is visible from the Two Bridges to Ashburton road, and two and a half miles from the former, a track runs north to the tor.

**LEATHER**  *Height above sea level: 1342 feet*
**TOR**  *Ordnance survey level: 564697*

Also known as Lader Tor it is very conspicuous standing as it does just north of the Burrator Reservoir and commands spectacular views over the same and to the country far to the south. It has an extensive clitter top and a kistvaen existed on its slopes. The tor is easily approached from the ring road around Burrator and passes its lower slopes at the northern part of the road.

**LEEDON**  *Height above sea level: 1277 feet*
**TOR**  *Ordnance survey level: 565717*

About three miles from Yelverton on the Princetown road it is visible from the same, and is notable for the blocks and slabs of granite sometimes called clatters found at its peak. On the western side will be found remains of an enclosure and hut circles. The old Princetown railway track lies on the west side. An extensive panoramic view can be enjoyed from the summit. A parking place exists three miles from Yelverton and access to the tor is quite easy.

| | |
|---|---|
| **LEGIS TOR** | *Height above sea level: 1000 feet*<br>*Ordnance survey reference: 569652* |

A most interesting tor with an unusual number of remains of prehistoric settlements. On its southern side will be found hut circle remains whilst on the western side a cairn and a stone row. The winding River Plym flows gently on its southern side. It is approached by locating Cadover bridge on the Yelverton to Ivybridge road. Following the river upstream for nearly two miles and Legis Tor will be found.

| | |
|---|---|
| **LITTLE HOUND TOR** | *Height above sea level: 1650 feet*<br>*Ordnance survey reference: 632890* |

Situated in the north of Dartmoor it is not very accessible being in the centre of a number of tors and is a long way from the nearest moorland track. It has a clitter top, a cairn and a stone circle on its north side. It is best approached from Throwleigh proceeding to Throwleigh Common continuing west and skirting Rayburrow Pool and Little Hound Tor will be discovered two miles from Throwleigh.

| | |
|---|---|
| **LITTLE KNEESET** | *Height above sea level: 1694 feet*<br>*Ordnance survey reference: 591843* |

In the centre of northern Dartmoor it is not of great historic importance and it is not very accessible. Two rivers start their course to the sea here, the Black Ridge Brook on its north side and the Cut Combe Water on the south side. It has a peat pass which indicates that peat for the length of the pass has been removed leaving a track. The tor is a mile and a half from Cranmere Pool and it is best approached from Okehampton by taking the road south and uphill past the railway station and on to the moor. Passing through the moor gate and following the road south as far as is possible, the peat pass must be located and which will lead to Little Kneeset.

| | |
|---|---|
| **LITTLE LINKS TOR** | *Height above sea level: 1924 feet*<br>*Ordnance survey reference: 549867* |

This is rather a small tor situated between Great Nodden and the Great Links Tors. It has a notable outcrop of rocks of unusual formation and in the vicinity can be found a cairn and hut circle remains. It lies a mile east of the *Fox and Hounds Inn* on the Tavistock to Okehampton road and a moorland track from the vicinity of the inn leads east to the lower slopes of the tor. It is in a danger area and notice should be taken of warning flags when flown.

| | |
|---|---|
| **LITTLE MISTOR** | *Height above sea level: 1591 feet*<br>*Ordnance survey reference: 565765* |

Situated in mid Dartmoor it is north of the Tavistock to Princetown road. It has a commanding view of the country to the south even to Plymouth sixteen miles to the south. To the west of the tor can be found enclosures, hut circles and rock basins. To the north lies Great Mistor. A track from Rundlestone on the above road leads to the tor. It is in a danger area and notice should be taken of warning flags when flown.

| | |
|---|---|
| **LINTS TOR** | *Height above sea level: 1710 feet*<br>*Ordnance survey reference: 580875* |

A small tor between the two highest parts of Dartmoor, and is a mile south of High Willhayes. The West Okement River and the Bren Brook pass on either side, east and west respectively. To reach it a track from Sourton on the Tavistock to Okehampton road leads to the base of Shelstone Tor north of which runs the West Okement. Following this river upstream one will find Lints Tor. It is in a danger area and notice should be taken of warning flags when flown.

## LITTAFORD TOR

*Height above sea level: 1400 feet*
*Ordnance survey reference: 615768*

A little north of Two Bridges this tor is a minor one being the southern point of the very high ground of central Dartmoor. It is close to Wistman's Wood and other than hut circles it provides much less prehistoric remains than the land to the north. It is approached from Two Bridges by following the Devonport Leat to its source and a further mile north will reach Littaford Tor.

## LONGAFORD TOR

*Height above sea level: 1550 feet*
*Ordnance survey reference: 615778*

The tor is found in mid Dartmoor north of Two Bridges. It has a clitter top and hut circles and enclosures can be found on the western side. South of the tor will be found the famous Wistman's Wood noted for its stunted trees. To find the tor start from Two Bridges and follow the Devonport Leat north for two miles.

## LOWER WHITE TOR

*Height above sea level: 1672 feet*
*Ordnance survey reference: 618793*

In the north of Dartmoor it twins with Higher White Tor. There is a little clitter at the top, but it is one of the lesser tors. To the north-west and clear of the marsh and bogland are the remains of enclosed hut circle groups. It is accessible from Archeton reached by a branch road north of the Tavistock to Okehampton road, one mile south-west of Postbridge. It lies in a danger area and notice should be taken of warning flags when flown.

## LYDFORD TOR

*Height above sea level: 1342 feet*
*Ordnance survey reference: 599782*

It is in mid Dartmoor just east of the Cowsic River, a tributary of the River Dart. To the north and west can be found the remains of an enclosure, hut circles and a stone row. The Beardown Man, a huge stone menhir some twelve feet high can be seen. It is approached from Two Bridges on the Tavistock to Okehampton road by following the Cowsic River to its source for two miles. It is a danger area and notice should be taken of warning flags when flown.

*Legis Tor:* One of the smallest stone circles on the moor.

**LYNCH TOR**  
*Height above sea level: 1696 feet*  
*Ordnance survey reference: 565806*

Has a clitter top and a cairn and hut circles to the west. The tor is approached from Peter Tavy by taking the Wapsworthy road and after leaving Wapsworthy continue on this road and take the first turning to the right. This leads to Bagga Tor and thence to Lynch Tor. It is in a danger area and notice should be taken when warning flags are flown.

**MEL TOR**  
*Height above sea level: 1450 feet*  
*Ordnance survey reference: 695725*

This tor is to be found north-west of Ashburton, and commands splendid views over the wooded banks of the River Dart and the moor to the west. It attracts many visitors as it is so close to the Ashburton to Princetown road, and will be found by using a track one and a half miles east of Dartmeet and this leads to the base of the tor.

**MELDON HILL**  
*Height above sea level: 1279 feet*  
*Ordnance survey reference: 696863*

About one mile south of Chagford and from its summit an excellent view of the surrounding countryside can be enjoyed. The road south and uphill from Chagford leads to the hill.

*Pew Tor:* An expansive view of its area and scattered rocks.

**MISTOR**  
*Height above sea level: 1431 feet*  
*Ordnance survey reference: 574757*

Situated in south-west Dartmoor and close to the Tavistock to Princetown road it is one of the lesser Mistors, Great Mistors and Little Mistor being the others. On the eastern side will be found Fice's Well believed by some to be of great age and having special healing effects when its water is used. The tor is reached by following the track north from Rundlestone on the above mentioned road.

**MERRIPIT HILL**  
*Height above sea level: 1473 feet*  
*Ordnance survey reference: 657804*

Stands on very high ground within half a mile of the road from Two Bridges to Moretonhampstead and one mile east of Postbridge. On it can be found a cist, a stone circle and row also hut circles. The road between Postbridge and Warren House does in fact climb steeply over the lower slopes of the hill and the peak is only a few hundred feet above the road level at the nearest point.

| | |
|---|---|
| **NAT**<br>**TOR** | *Height above sea level: 1000 feet*<br>*Ordnance survey reference: 544822* |

This tor is in west Dartmoor to the east of the River Tavy as it wends its way towards the sea, and further to the east an enclosure and hut circles can be found. To reach the tor proceed from Mary Tavy to Willsworthy a distance of two and a half miles, turn north for half a mile where a track leads direct to the tor.

| | |
|---|---|
| **NORTH HESSARY**<br>**TOR** | *Height above sea level: 1695 feet*<br>*Ordnance survey reference: 576742* |

This tor on the outskirts of Princetown and just west of it is noted for the high television mast standing on its summit which can be seen from many miles away. The old Princetown railway passed on its southern side and the quarry in which convicts from Dartmoor Prison laboured is to be seen on its eastern side, and the watch towers in which warders of the prison kept guard over the prisoners can still be seen. Finding the television mast is all that is necessary to locate the tor.

| | |
|---|---|
| **OKEMENT**<br>**HILL** | *Height above sea level: 1856 feet*<br>*Ordnance survey reference: 604877* |

It is situated in the northern part of Dartmoor in one of the most desolate parts. Although a barrow or burial ground is found on its slopes there is little other evidence of human activities. It is approached from Okehampton by proceeding south and uphill past the railway station and on to the moor. Passing through the moor gate and following the road south for three miles locates the Okement Hill.

| | |
|---|---|
| **PEW**<br>**TOR** | *Height above sea level: 1050 feet*<br>*Ordnance survey reference: 533736* |

East of Tavistock it has interesting rock formations and the evidence of a former quarry. On the northern side lies a very large stone evidently cut for some utility purpose, it is box shaped and perfectly cut in a rectangular manner, with true right angles. For what purpose? The tor is reached by crossing the Tavistock golf course by road and after leaving it take the first left hand turning which leads to the base of the tor.

| | |
|---|---|
| **PIL**<br>**TOR** | *Height above sea level: 1450 feet*<br>*Ordnance survey reference: 732758* |

Situated in east Dartmoor it is one of the minor tors. On the eastern side are to be found the Foales Arrishes. These are enclosures within which were hut circles. Access is best from Ashburton, proceeding north through Gold East Cross, and on to Hemsworthy Gate. The tor is half a mile east of this point.

| | |
|---|---|
| **RATTLEBROOK**<br>**HILL** | *Height above sea level: 1774 feet*<br>*Ordnance survey reference: 555853* |

In the north-west of Dartmoor it lies between Chat Tor and Great Links Tor. North-east of the tor are the remains of a disused mine. The tor is best approached from the *Dartmoor Inn* on the Tavistock to Okehampton road. A track from the spot leads east to the River Lyd. Following this river to its source leads to the western side of Rattlebrook. It is in a danger area and notice should be taken of warning flags when flown.

| | |
|---|---|
| **RIPPON**<br>**TOR** | *Height above sea level: 1560 feet*<br>*Ordnance survey reference: 747755* |

An interesting tor in east Dartmoor combining splendid views of south-east Devon with remains of a cairn, an enclosure and hut circles. Also of interest is a logan stone which comprises two large horizontal stones resting on top of a massive supporting stone. A road from Ashburton running north for a distance of four miles passes west of the Tor.

| **RIVAL** | *Height above sea level: 1350 feet* |
|---|---|
| **TOR** | *Ordnance survey reference: 645884* |

This is one of the minor tors adjacent to Buttern Hill, and although it is practically surrounded by marshes and bogs it has a stone circle on its north-east slopes and further north there are hut circle remains. The Walla Brook which runs into the River Teign passes south of the tor. Access is best from Chagford by taking the road to Gidleigh and then on to Berrydown. The Buttern Hill will have to be avoided by crossing the Gidleigh Common, and Rival Tor will be south-west of Buttern.

| **ROOK** | *Height above sea level: 1107 feet* |
|---|---|
| **TOR** | *Ordnance survey reference: 605617* |

This is a minor tor in south-west Dartmoor and is north of Cornwood and over which it has a splendid view. On the slopes and towards Shell Top can be found enclosures and hut circle remains. It is approached from Cornwood by taking the road north-east to Rook from where a track leads to Shell Top and Rook Tor.

| **ROOS** | *Height above sea level: 1410 feet* |
|---|---|
| **TOR** | *Ordnance survey reference: 549767* |

Otherwise known as Rolls Tor lies east of Cox Tor and north of Staple Tor. In the vicinity are the remains of rock basins, enclosures and hut circles, and it forms part of the Petertavy Great Common. It is easily found and from the *Merrivale Inn* on the Tavistock to Princetown road follow the river upstream for a mile and Roos Tor will be just to the west.

| **ROUGH** | *Height above sea level: 1580 feet* |
|---|---|
| **TOR** | *Ordnance survey reference: 607798* |

It lies at the very north of Dartmoor and is two miles south of Okehampton, and is has a clitter top. It is found by leaving Okehampton and proceeding south and uphill past the railway station and on to the moor. Passing through the moor gate follow the road for a mile and Rough Tor will be seen on the right hand side of the road.

| **ROUGH** | *Height above sea level: 1791 feet* |
|---|---|
| **TOR** | *Ordnance survey reference: 607798* |

Situated three miles north of Two Bridges on the Tavistock to Ashburton road and has no particular characteristics. The Devonport Leat rises one mile to the north and passes the tor on its eastern side. It is not of easy access, but starting at Two Bridges follow the Leat north past Crockern Tor, Littaford Tor and Wistman's Wood. Passing between Crow Tor and Higher White Tor and still following the Leat, Rough Tor will appear on the western side of it.

| **ROW** | *Height above sea level: 1375 feet* |
|---|---|
| **TOR** | *Ordnance survey reference: 594917* |

Row Tor is a clitter tor about two and a half miles from Okehampton. It is approached from Okehampton by proceeding south and uphill past the railway station and on to the moor. Leaving the Army camp on the right pass through the moor gate and follow the road for a mile and, at the first right hand junction, follow the road. Row Tor will be seen on the right. On the eastern slopes will be found the remains of St. Michael's Chapel and the crossing of the East Okement River is still called Chapleford.

| **ROYAL** | *Height above sea level: 1335 feet* |
|---|---|
| **HILL** | *Ordnance survey reference: 616727* |

Situated about two and a half miles south-east of Princetown it has interesting historical connections. The "Crock of Gold" is found on its northern slopes and was earlier associated with treasure and was called Money Pits and Gold Crocks. Kistvaens are to be found on the southern slopes. The tor is quite easy for access and at Princetown a moorland track runs south-east to Tor Royal where a left hand turn followed by a right hand turn will lead to the western side of the tor.

*Sharp Tor:* An impression as viewed from Yar Tor Down.

**SCAREY TOR**  *Height above sea level: 1280 feet*
*Ordnance survey reference: 606925*

It is in north Dartmoor and is less than one mile south-east of the hamlet of Belstone. To the south can be found the Cullever Steps and the Irishman's Wall. It is approached from Sticklepath on the Okehampton to Exeter road. Belstone lies one mile east and a moorland track around Watchet Hill leads to Scarey Tor one mile further to the south-west. It is subject to use by the military and notice should be taken of warning flags when flown.

**SCORHILL TOR**  *Height above sea level: 1350 feet*
*Ordnance survey reference: 658872*

Nearly three miles west of Chagford with the North Teign River passing immediately south of the tor, it has a clitter top and is notable for the Scorhill Circle which Samuel Rowe in *Perambulations of Dartmoor* describes it as the most complete specimen of a sacred circle in the county. It is approached from Chagford by taking the road to Gidleigh and Berrydown and from here the tor is easily accessible.

**SHAPLEY TOR**  *Height above sea level: 1598 feet*
*Ordnance survey reference: 698821*

Situated in north-east Dartmoor it is part of a ridge of high ground including King Tor, Hameldown Tor and Hameldown Beacon. Remains of hut circles are to be found on the north side and to the south there are stone rows. The tor is one mile from Two Bridges on the Moretonhampstead road, and four miles from the latter a road south leads direct to Shapley Tor.

**SHARP TOR**  *Height above sea level: 1215 feet*
*Ordnance survey reference: 686730*

A very prominent tor having a clitter or clatter peak and is situated a mile west of the River Dart. On the eastern slopes which rise steeply from the river will be found remains of hut circles. Its highest point gives an excellent viewpoint of the River Dart. Access is best made by proceeding up the steep hill from Dartmeet eastwards towards Ashburton for a mile and a half where a track to the right will lead to the eastern slope of the tor.

**SHARP TOR**  *Height above sea level: 1370 feet*
*Ordnance survey reference: 650617*

One of the southern tors of Dartmoor it lies about four miles north of Bittaford on the Plymouth to Ivybridge road. It has an enclosure, a cairn and hut circles on its slopes. It is found by following a track north from Bittaford around Ugborough Beacon and proceeding still north for two and a half miles when Sharp Tor will be seen on the western side.

**SHARP TOR**  *Height above sea level: 1340 feet*
*Ordnance survey reference: 551848*

This is one of several tors with the same name although one or more of the others are known as Sharpitor. It is situated on the north-west boundary of Dartmoor and is central to three tors in close proximity, Chat Tor to the north and Hare Tor to the south. On the western slopes are the remains of a cairn and hut circles on the eastern slope. It is about two miles east of the *Dartmoor Inn* on the Tavistock to Okehampton road and is best approached from the Willsworthy Camp on the same road from which a track leads north-east to the tor. It is in a danger area and notice should be taken of warning flags when flown.

**SHARPITOR**  *Height above sea level: 1320 feet*
*Ordnance survey reference: 559703*

Located about three miles from Yelverton on the Princetown road it is very prominent. Reaching the top of the very long and steep Peak Hill one will notice a moorland pond just east of the road. This point is a favourite rendezvous for the wild ponies and also a popular parking place for motorists. Sharpitor is just half a mile east and a glorious panoramic view is obtained from the summit.

**SHAVERCOMBE TOR**  *Height above sea level: 1200 feet*
*Ordnance survey reference: 595664*

This tor is in an area full of Dartmoor history. The River Plym passes its northern slopes and past workings of tinners can be seen over a large area. Hut circles, enclosures, stone rows and cairns are numerous and yet looking to the east one has the feeling that the moor has remained unaltered for thousands of years. It is approached from Yelverton via Sheepstor village on to Gutter Tor, and skirting the latter leads to Ditsworthy Warren which is south-east of the tor. Shavercombe then lies across the River Plym which is easily crossed.

*Sheepstor:* A very prominent and accessible tor close to Burrator.

### SHEEPSTOR
*Height above sea level: 1050 feet*
*Ordnance survey reference: 565683*

Otherwise known as Shidford and Shittestowe, is one of the most prominent of all the tors. Four miles east of Yelverton it overshadows the Burrator and the Sheepstor hamlets. A cave is said to exist here and it is said the members of an Elford family took refuge in it in the days of the Civil War. Amidst the huge bounders on the southern side there is plenty of scope for a search of this cave. Remains of hut circles can be found in Yellowmead on the eastern side of the tor. It is reached by following the road from Dousland to Burrator and continuing on to Sheepstor village where the tor will be seen to dominate the area.

### SHELL TOP
*Height above sea level: 1557 feet*
*Ordnance survey reference: 598638*

This is one of the highest points of south Dartmoor and splendid views to the south can be enjoyed. On its western slopes can be found the remains of a barrow and hut circle groups. It is approached from the Yelverton to Ivybridge road. Two miles south-east of Cadover Bridge on this road will be found a track to the obvious Shell Top to the east.

### SHELSTONE TOR
*Height above sea level: 1050 feet*
*Ordnance survey reference: 557898*

Situated in the north-west of Dartmoor it has a clitter top. The West Okement River flows past its eastern slope, and on the south, towards Bransombe Loaf, the remains of a cairn can be found. Access is best from Sourton on the Tavistock to Okehampton road and a moorland track passing Sourton Tors will lead to the base of the tor.

### SITTAFORD TOR
*Height above sea level: 1763 feet*
*Ordnance survey reference: 634831*

Found in mid Dartmoor it is associated with Grey Withers the largest stone circle on the moor, and has a small amount of clitter on its summit. It is west of the Fernworthy Forest, but it is thought that the best approach is from Postbridge by following the East River Dart to its source and which is on the southern slopes of the tor.

### SOURTON TOR
*Height above sea level: 1444 feet*
*Ordnance survey reference: 544896*

Situated one mile east of Sourton, and from the summit an extensive view of the west extending into Cornwall can be enjoyed. It is found from Sourton on the Tavistock to Okehampton road by a moorland track running east which leads to its western slope.

### SOUTH DOWN
*Height above sea level: 1227 feet*
*Ordnance survey reference: 555913*

Situated on the eastern side of Dartmoor it is visible from the Two Bridges to Dartmeet road. It is notable for its crosses which probably marked the route which monks followed in travelling across the moor. On the northern slopes can be found the remains of hut circles and an enclosure. A stream rises on the hill and makes its way to the Dart River. It is best approached from Hexworthy and a distance of a mile and a half across the moor in a south-west direction and the hill is reached.

### SOUTH HESSARY TOR
*Height above sea level: 1410 feet*
*Ordnance survey reference: 597724*

Standing to the south of Princetown it is of lesser height than North Hessary Tor. To the west are remains of hut circles otherwise there is little of importance connected with this tor. Access is easy. From Princetown a moorland road east from the Square leads to Tor Royal and following the track to the right and south will bring one to the eastern side of the tor.

**STANDON HILL**  
*Height above sea level: 1600 feet*  
*Ordnance survey reference: 555815*

Rises steeply from the River Tavy to the west. The remains of a cairn, hut circles and an enclosure can be found. An excellent view of the country in the Mary Tavy district can be had from the summit. The tor is found by approaching from Peter Tavy and taking the road to Wapsworthy and continuing on and into the moor where a track will end on the lower slopes of the hill.

**STANNON TOR**  
*Height above sea level: 1150 feet*  
*Ordnance survey reference: 645815*

Standing on the high ground above Postbridge it commands very fine views to the south. Remains of beehive hut circles exist to the north. To reach the tor follow the East Dart River to its source from Postbridge for a distance of a mile and a half.

**STAPLE TORS**  
*Height above sea level: 1493 feet*  
*Ordnance survey reference: 542757*

This tor has two separate clitter or rock formations, the most notable being south of the peak. Here the rocks form unusual pillars of stone piled horizontally on top of each other to a height of more than twenty feet. The tor lies just north of Merrivale on the Tavistock to Princetown road and is easily approached from this road being less than a mile north of it. An excellent car park exists within easy access.

**STONETOR HILL**  
*Height above sea level: 1400 feet*  
*Ordnance survey reference: 647858*

This tor is very prominent from the Tavistock to Okehampton road and is only one mile from the inn at Sourton Down, and a track east from the main road leads to the western slopes of the tor.

**TER HILL**  
*Height above sea level: 1575 feet*  
*Ordnance survey reference: 642707*

A minor tor where a tributary of the North Teign River rises and is north of the Fenworthy Forest. It has enclosures and hut circles on both its northern and southern sides. It is not very accessible being four miles from the nearest main road. However a road west from Chagford to Teigncombe and Batworthy and crossing Shoven Down leads to Stonetor.

**THORNWORTHY TOR**  
*Height above sea level: 1720 feet*  
*Ordnance survey reference: 665853*

Situated in north-east Dartmoor it is just north of the Fernworthy Reservoir. It has a clitter top; on the north side can be found stone rows and a cist whilst on the eastern side are hut circle remains. The South Teign River flows in a northerly direction past the east side of the tor. Access is best from Chagford by taking the road to Thorn thence through Frenchbeer from which a track leads to the lower slopes of the tor.

**TOR ROYAL**  
*Height above sea level: 1200 feet*  
*Ordnance survey reference: 605732*

A little more than a mile east of Princetown from which it is easily accessible. On the northern slopes are the remains of a cairn and on the east side is the Crock of Gold cist. The Abbotts' Way which was a path taken by Monks across the moor from Buckfastleigh to Princetown thence to Tavistock passes on the west side. From the Square at Princetown a track east leads direct to Tor Royal.

**TROWELSWORTHY TOR**  
*Height above sea level: 1141 feet*  
*Ordnance survey reference: 579644*

This is a tor above the Plym valley in an area rich in prehistoric remains. To the north will be found enclosures and hut circles, whilst to the south remains of stone rows and a circle can be seen. The area is a noted picnic spot as it is easily reached. The tor is just over a mile from Cadover Bridge on the Yelverton to Ivybridge road and there is a parking area from which the tor and the whole area may be visited.

### WATERN TOR

*Height above sea level: 1750 feet*
*Ordnance survey reference: 628864*

This is a very conspicuous tor in the north of Dartmoor. An interesting feature is that two separate layers are formed through which a passage exists. Hut circles, a barrow, and a kistvaen can be found. It is not easily accessible but it is best approached from Okehampton. Proceeding south and uphill past the railway station the moor is entered, passing through the moor gate a track will lead to within one mile of the tor. It is in a danger area and notice should be taken of warning flags when flown.

### WEST MILL TOR

*Height above sea level: 1700 feet*
*Ordnance survey reference: 586910*

Situated in the north of Dartmoor it lies just east of High Willhayes the highest point in the south of England. It has a clitter summit and the Red-a-Ven Brook starts its journey on the lower slopes. It is approached from Okehampton by going south and uphill past the railway station and on to the moor. Pass through the moor gate, a mile from which will be found a road junction. A turn to the right and a further half a mile and the foot of the tor is reached. It is in a danger area and notice should be taken of warning flags when flown.

*Watern Tor:* A graphic illustration of granite rock formations.

### WHITE HILL

*Height above sea level: 1279 feet*
*Ordnance survey reference: 534839*

This hill or tor is one of the most western of the Dartmoor tors and is only one mile east of the Tavistock to Okehampton road. There is a tumuli on the west side and hut circles on the east side between it and Hare Tor. It is approached from Willsworthy Camp where a moorland track leads direct to the hill.

### WHITE TOR

*Height above sea level: 1527 feet*
*Ordnance survey reference: 543784*

The summit of the rising ground east of the River Tavy is rich in prehistoric remains. There is evidence of hut circles a camp and cairns. On the summit are two rows of stones placed horizontally above one another and they have led to speculation as to whether they were constructed by man or natural elements. Access is fairly easy, by using a road from Peter Tavy east to Boulters Tor, passing around the same and proceeding direct to the Tor. It is in a danger area and notice should be taken of warning flags when flown.

*Vixen Tor:* A prominent rock stack overlooking the Walkham valley.

**WHITEHORSE HILL**

*Height above sea level: 1973 feet*
*Ordnance survey reference: 616854*

This is one of the highest hills or tors on Dartmoor and locates the Taw Head which becomes the River Taw and flows north, and the East Dart Head which flows south and becomes the River Dart, yet there is barely half a mile between the sources of these two rivers. It is very close to the Cranmere Pool the object of many ramblers who explore the moors. It is not very accessible, but starting from Okehampton take the road south and uphill past the railway station and on to the moor. Pass through the moor gate and follow the road south as far as is possible. This will bring one to Hangstone Hill and Whitehorse Hill is half a mile south. It is in a danger area and notice should be taken when warning flags are flown.

**WILD TOR**

*Height above sea level: 1741 feet*
*Ordnance survey reference: 623878*

A tor with a great amount of clitter, with a barrow or burying ground in the area. The Walla Brook rises near Hangstone Hill to the south. An adventurous way to approach it is from Chagford, by proceeding to Gidleigh thence to Gidleigh Common. Follow the Walla Brook for two miles when Wild Tor will be reached. It is in a danger area and notice should be taken of warning flags when flown.

**WIND TOR**

*Height above sea level: 1020 feet*
*Ordnance survey reference: 707758*

It rises sharply and west of the Webburn River, a tributary of the River Dart. It provides an excellent viewpoint of the wooded area to the south and Buckfastleigh. Hut circle remains can be found in the area. It is approached from Ponsworthy half a mile east of Two Bridges on the Ashburton road. From Ponsworthy a road north-west will lead to Dunstone which is on the east side of Wind Tor.

**WINTER TOR**

*Height above sea level: 1400 feet*
*Ordnance survey reference: 609915*

One of the lesser tors it is two and a half miles south-west of Okehampton. It is approached from Okehampton by proceeding south and uphill past the railway station and on to the moor. Pass through the moor gate and follow the track for two and a half miles in a south-east direction and the base of the tor is reached. It is in a danger area and notice should be taken of warning flags when flown.

**VIXEN TOR**

*Height above sea level: 1050 feet*
*Ordnance survey reference: 543743*

Unlike most tors, Vixen is a series of rock masses piled on one another in three formations and it rises on slopes forming the valley of the Walkham River. It is plainly visible from the Tavistock to Princetown road from which it has a sphinx-like appearance. The most interesting approach is from Sampford Spinney crossing the moor in a northerly direction for two miles. It is emphasised that the moorland to the west of the tor is bogland and should be avoided at all times.

**YAR TOR**

*Height above sea level: 1405 feet*
*Ordnance survey level: 677741*

Stands in a position dominating Dartmeet and on its summit remains of a kistvaen, a barrow and a stone row can be found. It is immediately north-east of Dartmeet on the Two Bridges to Ashburton road and access is possible from the parking area at this point.

**YES TOR**

*Height above sea level: 2030 feet*
*Ordnance survey reference: 581903*

The second highest of the tors it is not easily accessible from the Tavistock to Okehampton road. Tumuli or burial grounds exist on the east slopes. The easiest approach route is from Okehampton by proceeding south and uphill past the railway station and on to the moor. Proceed through the moor gate and bear left just after crossing the Moor Brook. The tor is about one and a half miles south of this point. It is in a danger area and notice should be taken of warning flags when flown.

*Yar Tor:* A fortress like formation at the summit of Yar Hill.

# GLOSSARY

*BARROW:* A mount of stones or earth or both to mark a place of burial.
*CAIRNS or CISTS:* A collection of stones lying on the ground to denote a burial place.
*CLITTER:* A natural formation of rock crowning the peak of a tor.
*CLATTER:* Formations of huge slabs and rocks lying on the side of a tor.
*ENCLOSURE:* An area surrounded by vertical stones to form a compound but is better known as a Pound.
*HUT CIRCLES:* These are the ruins or remains of prehistoric dwellings. The walls only remain standing now and form an approximate circle varying from seven feet to twenty eight feet across.
*KISTVAEN:* A rectangular formation of stones set in the ground with a top covering stone. Average length five feet and width two feet; denotes a burial place.
*LOGAN STONE:* These are very large stones resting horizontally on one or more vertical stones.
*ROCK BASINS:* Hollows in granite usually retaining water.
*MENHIRS:* Large vertical stones erected as monuments and sometimes reaching twelve feet in height.
*STONE ROWS:* Vertical stones sunk into the ground at varying distances apart to form a straight line.
*TUMULI:* Burial grounds.

## The Use of the Ordnance Survey Map

The references in this book are taken from the appropriate survey map and consist of six figures.

The first three figures called "Eastings" refer to the figures at the top and bottom of the map which run from left to right. The first two figures give guidance to the square involved and the third number is the number of tenths of the location before the next Easting number.

Example 1.

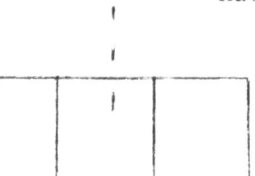

X gives a reading 525 and all points north of this point will have the same reading.

Similarly the figures called "Northings" are found on the extreme edges of the map running south to north.

Example 2.

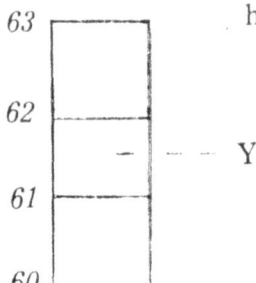

Y gives a reading 615 and all points east of this point will have the same reading.

Thus given a reference of 525615 select a point 525 as above and 615 ditto. Projecting these two points north and east the map reference 525615 is determined.

To find the map reference of a given point reverse the above operation.

# Tors of Dartmoor Addendum 2026

*By Paul Rendell*

Since this book was first published in the 1980s, a lot of things have changed on Dartmoor.

A number of tors were listed as being in the live firing range but this is not the case. Arms Tor, Belstone Tor, Brat Tor, Cox Tor, Crow Tor, Doe Tor, Little Mis Tor, Lower White Tor, Scarey Tor, White Tor, and Winter Tor are all outside the firing ranges.

There is spelling mistake on page 3 – Arms Tor, it should read Shortacombe, not Shartacombe.

P3 – Baggator. The last paragraph relates to Bag Tor, also known as Bog Tor on East Dartmoor and not Baggator on West Dartmoor.

P4 - Bel Tor. This tor on private land and there is no access but can be seen from the car park at Bel Tor corner.

P6 – Buckland Beacon. You will find the Ten Commandments stones on Buckland Beacon and best place to park at Cold East Cross, where there is a car park.

P7 – Calveslake Tor is near the source but not at the source.

P7 – Cawsand Beacon is better known today as Cosdon Beacon.

P7 – Chat Tor is within the firing range.

P9 – Criptor is on private land.

P11 – Flat Tor. The position of Flat Tor was misplaced for many years by the OS. It is now at SX 608 815.

P12 – Great Kneeset Tor – The military ring road was closed many years ago, so following the road to its most southerly point is only now by on path, not by a vehicle.

P13 – Gren Tor. It should read Shortacombe, not Shartacombe.

P15 – Hartor Tors. Lower and Higher Hart Tor - you do not have to cross the river to visit these tors.

P17 – Hockington Tor. The grid ref is more near SX 695 719.

P18 – Hound Tor. There are two Hound Tors on Dartmoor. The author has mixed up the two tors. The Hound Tor on north Dartmoor has the grid ref does have clitter and does not have huge piles of granite as high as seventy feet. This is the tor on East Dartmoor, near Haytor.

P19 – Kitty Tor. It should read Shortacombe, not Shartacombe.

P20 – Little Kneesett Tor. The military ring road was closed many years ago, so following the road to its most southerly point is only now on path, not by a vehicle.

P23 – Nat Tor is within the firing range.

P23 – Okement Hill. The military ring road was closed many years ago, so you can no longer drive there, you have to walk along the track. Also it is within the firing range.

P23 – Pil Tor – it should read Cold East Cross, not Gold East Cross.

P23 – Rippon Tor. The logan stone is no longer there.

P24 – Row Tor is within the firing range.

P28 – Standon Hill is within the firing range.

P28 – Ter Hill. The text should be for Stonetor Hill.

P28 - Ter Hill- the grid is for Ter Hill but there no tor here. None of the text on this matches Ter Hill anyway.

P29 – White Hill. There is no outcrop on this hill. Willsworthy Camp has now been moved.

P30 – Whitehorse Hill. There is no outcrop of here. The military ring road was closed many years ago, so you can no longer drive there, you have walk along the track.

P31 – Vixen Tor. This tor now is private, no access to the tor.

Paul Rendell Local historian and editor of Dartmoor News

Thanks are given to Paul Rendell for providing both updates and corrections to the original text, ensuring that this book can continue to be enjoyed. I made the decision to publish the main content of the book without alterations to preserve the 'historical' integrity of the republishing project. I am not a local historian, nor am I a Dartmoor expert, so any alteration to a book is not taken lightly. Knowing I had an expert available to provide some much needed additions was hugely helpful and I am very grateful for the time he gave to reading and updating the information.

Steven Gibson, 2026

# Arthur L. Clamp – the man behind the books

Arthur Leslie Clamp was a man of boundless energy with a passion for helping others, particularly through his love of history. A printer by trade, he started his career in a printing company before moving his family from Exeter to Plymouth to teach at the Plymouth College of Art and Design, where he eventually became the Head of the Printing Department.

*Arthur with his five children.*

## A Devoted Family Man

Despite his love of teaching, Arthur prioritised his family, always making it home by 5:30pm for tea. He and his wife, Rosemary, raised five children: Susan, Angela, Elizabeth, David, and Steven. Arthur would often combine his love of family and history by taking his children on Sunday walks, encouraging them to appreciate historical monuments by taking photos or making crayon rubbings of gravestones for his books. The family home at 203 Elburton Road was a hub of activity, with a large garden, featuring a two-storey fort and a makeshift swimming pool.

## A Lifelong Learner and Adventurer

Arthur's thirst for knowledge extended beyond history to a deep curiosity about the world. He was passionate about exploring different cultures, traditions, and cuisines, often taking advantage of his long summer holidays as a teacher to travel to places like India, Russia, South America, the middle east and the USA, sometimes bringing one of his children along. This adventurous spirit even influenced his home life, as seen by the short-lived family tradition of steam-cooking vegetables after a trip to Iceland.

*History is a prominent feature of family days out*

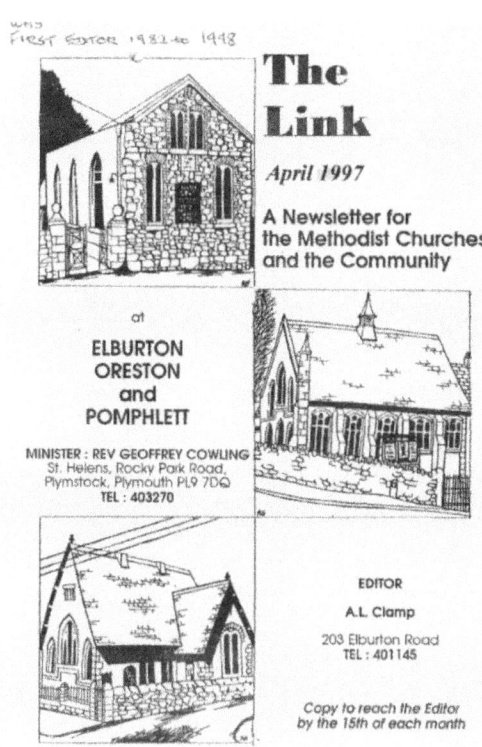

## Community and Philanthropic Spirit

His commitment to serving others was evident in his long-standing involvement with the Elburton Methodist Church. He was the Sunday School Superintendent for over 15 years and served as the editor of the wider church's monthly newsletter, "The Link," for a similar duration. After Rosemary's very sad passing, Arthur later remarried and, following a chance encounter with a professor from India, established a connection with a missionary school in Chennai. Together with his new wife, Christine, he co-founded a "Sponsor a Child's Education" program that continues to this day.

*Pictured left – The cover of 'The Link' complete
with hand drawn sketches of each church by Angela
Below right – Arthur Clamp promoting his latest book
Below left – Arthur at home with his first wife, Rosemary
Below centre – Arthur on holiday with his second wife, Christine*

## A Legacy of Learning and Positivity

Arthur's greatest passion was history, which he brought to life through tireless research, documentation, and the many books he authored. He was driven by a need to "never be stuck in a rut," constantly seeking new experiences, meeting new people, and expanding his knowledge. With a positive attitude and a great sense of humour, he was always ready to help others, leaving a lasting impact on his family and community. His children, Susan, Angela, Elizabeth, David, and Steven, remember him with love and gratitude.

David Clamp, 2025

## A Legacy of Local History

Below is the story of how Arthur L Clamp began writing books, in his own words, drafted shortly before he passed away in 2001. I have only made minor alterations to this text, correcting grammatical errors that he did not survive to correct himself. When I first discovered this text, I was shocked to see my name mentioned. It seems that, unbeknownst to me, I shared my first PC with him. I suspect he used it during the day when I was at school, although I do have one memory of sitting with him and showing him how it worked. It has been a pleasure to pick up where he left off and see his books republished and redistributed, and to know that I was part of the story, even back then. It was also fascinating to discover that his pricing structure matches the way I have tried to price the books, with a third going to local sellers and the rest covering printing costs with a little left over for my expenses.

I am his eldest grandson, and it is a privilege to curate his legacy, which we are calling 'The Clamp Collection'. The very last line of the text originally reads "The following pages list all the titles." Sadly, that page is missing and we have no record of all the books he published and knowing that some of those were researched by other authors makes the process of finding them even harder. I look forward to one day completing the collection and seeing them all available again. And maybe, one day, I'll even start writing my own to add to the series. For now, here is his story in his own words.

Steven Gibson, 2025

## Writing and Publishing Booklets on Local Topics and Areas

I started this interest in either 1968 or 1969 when living in Woodford. I had by these dates established the Department of Printing and I think I must have been looking for something different to do. The first titles were of A5 size proofed from type set at Clarke, Doble and Brendon, Ltd., Plymouth printers, and then made up into pages and printed at Sawtell and Neilson, Ltd., Totnes.

Then began a slow process of getting them out to shops, etc. which proved to be more time consuming and difficult than actually researching, writing and getting the books into print. However, I persisted and opened a business account with Barclays Bank on the Broadway. I was advised to give it a title so I called it "Westway Publications". There came along another problem, one of storage of paper and finished books which was solved when the family moved to Elburton in 1970.

I changed the printer to Penwell, Ltd., Callington, Cornwall, as he was then just setting up himself and his prices seemed very reasonable. I did not get any of the printers to make up the complete books. I hand folded the flat printed sheets, stitched the books on a small manual table stitcher and trimmed them in a small hand turned guillotine which I bought from someone in Penzance for £40. It was brought up in a van.

The trouble and time going to and fro to Callington was too much so I transferred the printing to PDS Printers, Prince Rock, Plymouth, and I have been with them ever since. Now they are at Plympton which is easy to reach and they fold the flat sheets which was turning out to be a long chore which only saved a small part of the printing costs.

All my first titles were written by myself. I took the photographs and developed them in the loft of the house, the type was set by now on a computer situated in the house at Elburton from which I had collected photographic lengths of text to cut up and law down as pages.

At some point I decided that I would do my own film processing of lith film so I bought a large second hand process camera from Kingsbridge and learnt through trial and error to make line negatives of the text and halftone negatives of the illustrations which proved more difficult than I anticipated. The main problem was trying to keep the developer in the large dish at the correct temperature as any change would affect the developing time. I replaced this old camera with a brand new one bought from Croydon, Surrey, costing £900. This has turned out to be a great asset cutting out an expensive part of the printer's costs and one crucial aspect of the work which I could control.

By the middle 1970s there were many outlets I had contacted in Plymouth, up to Dartmoor, Exeter, around to Torbay, Totnes, Dartmouth and the South Hams. The market for local books was much greater than I had first thought and through getting to know many local people undertaking research themselves had the chance to help and make up books for other people who had in most instances, got together a collection of photographs with some text in a rather muddled way. Through my experience in print I was able to shape up their work and get it into print and in every case I had to pay the printer and let the person have the royalties. In the majority of titles produced in this manner this was another way of producing titles and it did give some profit to my work. However, I must say that in a few cases I lost out by either the other person getting the numbers wrong, not returning any monies from stock I delivered or they thought that more of their books should have been sold.

The print run was usually 1,000 copies and from time to time I have had reprints of 250 copies. It took about ten years to clear the first print run so I always had large stocks in the garage, workshop, etc. The numbers sold during the early years was about 7,000 copies a year increasing to around 9,000 copies and for the whole of the enterprise about 500,000 have been sold. The booklets have become part of the local scene and many people collect them, shops regularly order copies and I go around certain areas month by month restocking or replacing titles as necessary.

During the past year or so I have started setting the text on a Packard Bell PC, something which I should have done some years back. I share it with Steven Gibson, my grandson. There appears to be no end to the market for local books, but I could not earn a regular income because of the long time it takes to sell stock.

However, now exceeding 100 titles made up mainly of A4 twenty-four page booklets, some folded guides, with selling prices set with a third going to the shop which is the trade custom, the original idea has been quite successful and could go on for ever.

Apart from monetary benefits, however spasmodically these might be, I have learnt a lot myself, met many interesting people and have become part of the local scene with requests to give talks and to advise people about getting into print.

Arthur L Clamp, 2001

This newspaper article, published by the Evening Herald on 17th August 2001, forms a good record of his life. Just as he encourages us to learn more about local history, we encourage you to learn a little about him. For that reason, we have included these pages at the back of all the most recently republished books, in honour of his memory and recognition of his contribution to the community.

www.ingramcontent.com/pod-product-compliance
Lightning Source LLC
Chambersburg PA
CBHW061405070526
44584CB00031B/4168